First Facts®

MY FIRST GUIDE TO

MILITARY VEHICLES

by Kathryn Clay

WITHDRAWN

CAPSTONE PRESS
a capstone imprint

First Facts are published by Capstone Press,
1710 Roe Crest Drive, North Mankato, Minnesota 56003
www.capstonepub.com

Library of Congress Cataloging-in-Publication Data
Clay, Kathryn.
  My first guide to military vehicles / by Kathryn Clay.
      pages cm.—(First facts. My first guides)
  Includes bibliographical references and index.
  Summary: "Simple text and large, colorful photographs introduce young readers to various
military vehicles"–Provided by publisher.
  Audience: Grades K–3.
  ISBN 978-1-4914-2050-8 (library binding)
  ISBN 978-1-4914-2256-4 (ebook PDF)
1. Transportation, Military—Juvenile literature. 2. Vehicles, Military—Juvenile literature. I. Title
  UC270.C53 2015
  623.74—dc23   2014032619

Editorial Credits
Alesha Sullivan, editor; Tracy McCabe, designer; Jo Miller, media researcher; Katy LaVigne,
production specialist

Photo Credits
iStockphotos: rockfinder, cover; U.S. Air Force photo by Master Sgt. Jeremy Lock, 11 (top), Senior
Master Sgt. John S. Chapman, 9 (top); U.S. Army National Guard photo by Sgt. Adam Simmler,
21 (bottom); U. S. Army photo by Capt. John Farmer, 5; U. S. Marine Corps photo by Cpl. D.
J. Wu, 7; U. S. Navy photo by Alan Antczak, 21 (top), Cmdr. Erik Etz, 11 (bottom), CPO Daniel
Taylor, 19, MC1 Lynn Friant, 13, PO2 Michael Lavender, 9 (bottom), PO2 Miguel Contreras, 15
(bottom), Seaman Harry Andrew D. Gordon, 15 (top), courtesy of General Dynamics Electric
Boat, 17

Design Elements
Shutterstock: ExpressVectors, Jiri Vaclavek, MaKars, MisterElements, Nik Merkulov

Printed in the United States of America in North Mankato, Minnesota.
092014   008482CGS15

TABLE OF CONTENTS

MILITARY MACHINES IN ACTION

Military vehicles travel by land, air, and ocean. Tanks rumble over rough ground. Fighter jets chase after enemy aircrafts. Submarines stay hidden while sneaking under the water.

Although they have differences, each vehicle has the same goal. They help keep **civilians** and military members safe.

civilian—a person who is not in the military

TANKS

Tanks search for and destroy enemy targets. A tank's heavy **armor** protects the crew inside of the tank. Today the military uses the M1, M1A1, and M1A2.

The M109 howitzer looks like a tank, but it's really a rolling cannon. Its giant **artillery** can fire at enemy targets up to 19 miles (31 kilometers) away.

armor—a protective metal covering
artillery—cannons and other large guns used during battles

turret

main gun

road wheels

track

M1A1

HUMVEES AND MRAPs

Humvees are usually faster than tanks and cheaper to fix. They carry weapons and troops. Large, armored Humvees protect smaller vehicles.

Mine Resistant Ambush Protected (MRAP) vehicles are even tougher than Humvees. They are made to hold up better if hit by small explosives.

Humvee—High Mobility Multipurpose Wheeled Vehicle (HMMWV)

gunner station

squad box

armored plating

engine

MRAP

FIGHTER JETS AND BOMBERS

Fighter jets speed through the skies. They turn, lift, and dive while shooting down enemy planes. The jets also may carry bombs to attack ground targets.

Bombers are made just to hit targets on the ground. The B-52 Stratofortress drops bombs that crush **bunkers**. The bombs crash through concrete walls before exploding.

bunker—an underground shelter from bomb attacks and gunfire

F-22 Raptor
Fighter Jet

cockpit

bombs

F/A-18C Hornet

FACT

F-22 Raptor jets fly up to Mach 2. Mach 2
is 1,522 miles (2,449 kilometers) per hour.
That's twice the speed of sound!

11

HELICOPTERS

Helicopters can do a variety of jobs. The SH-60 Seahawk performs search and rescue missions. The AH-64 Apache and AH-64D Longbow are Army attack helicopters.

The CH-53E Super Stallion carries troops to new areas. It can hold about 40 Marines.

FACT

Unlike airplanes, helicopters can take off and land vertically. They can stay in one spot or fly low to the ground.

SH-60 Seahawk

ON THE WATER

Aircraft carriers are like small cities floating on the sea. The 3,000 sailors and 2,500 **airmen** aboard are able to respond quickly to new threats.

Destroyers protect U.S. shores. *Arleigh Burke* destroyers are some of the largest Navy ships. They carry about 270 crew members.

airman—a member of the Air Force

aircraft carrier

control tower

flight deck

control tower

helicopter landing area

hull

Arleigh Burke destroyer

FACT

Aircraft carriers have four catapults. The catapults on aircraft carriers propel airplanes to 165 miles (266 kilometers) per hour in two seconds!

SUBMARINES

Submarines act as secret underwater guards. They run on **nuclear** power, which is quiet and long lasting.

Attack submarines carry missiles, torpedoes, and mines to fight enemy subs and ships. Some submarines also carry nuclear warheads.

nuclear—having to do with the energy created by splitting atoms; nuclear bombs use this energy to cause an explosion; nuclear reactors on subs use this energy as a power source

masts

diving rudders

escape hatch

attack submarine

CROSSOVERS

Crossover vehicles are like two vehicles in one. The Light Amphibious Resupply Cargo (LARC) vehicle can travel on both land and water. The LARC-5 mainly hauls supplies to shore.

The Landing Craft Air Cushion (LCAC) is a **hovercraft** that can travel more than 50 miles (80 kilometers) per hour. An LCAC is big and can carry an entire tank.

hovercraft—a vehicle that travels on a cushion of air over both land and water

LARC vehicle

UNMANNED VEHICLES

Some military vehicles can travel without drivers. Operators tell them what to do with a remote control. The vehicles can watch enemies and explode mines while the operators are far away from danger. Unmanned vehicles can also shoot bullets and launch grenades.

remote controlled unmanned vehicle

PackBot

Glossary

airman (AYR-man)—a member of the Air Force

armor (AR-muhr)—a protective metal covering

artillery (ar-TIL-uh-ree)—cannons and other large guns used during battles

bunker (BUHNG-kuhr)—an underground shelter from bomb attacks and gunfire

civilian (si-VIL-yuhn)—a person who is not in the military

hovercraft (HUHV-ur-kraft)—a vehicle that travels on a cushion of air over both land and water

Humvee (HUHM-vee)—High Mobility Multipurpose Wheeled Vehicle (HMMWV)

nuclear (NOO-klee-ur)—having to do with the energy created by splitting atoms; nuclear bombs use this energy to cause an explosion; nuclear reactors on subs use this energy as a power source

Read More

Cohn, Jessica. *Military Machines*. Machines in Motion. New York: Gareth Stevens Publishing, 2014.

Colson, Rob. *Tanks and Military Vehicles*. Ultimate Machines. New York: PowerKids Press, 2013.

Shank, Carol. *U.S. Military Assault Vehicles*. U.S. Military Technology. North Mankato, Minn.: Capstone Press, 2013.

Internet Sites

FactHound offers a safe, fun way to find Internet sites related to this book. All of the sites on FactHound have been researched by our staff.

Here's all you do:

Visit *www.facthound.com*

Type in this code: 9781491420508

Check out projects, games and lots more at
www.capstonekids.com

Critical Thinking Using the Common Core

1. How do unmanned vehicles keep civilians and military members safe? (Key Ideas and Details)

2. Look at the military vehicles in the photo on page 5. What is the link between this photo and the main text? (Craft and Structure)

Index